What the Jews Believe

What th

Jews Believe

BY PHILIP S. BERNSTEIN

Illustrated by Fritz Eichenberg

Farrar, Straus and Young·
New York

Manufactured in the United States of America by H. Wolff, New York. Designed by Stefan Salter.

First Printing, March 1951
Second Printing, April 1951

Contents

What the Jews Believe

What the Jews Believe

*W*HAT do Jews, here and now, believe? To answer this question is the purpose of this book. We reluctantly turn our gaze from the rich patterns of Jewish life in other lands and times, and direct our attention to the living faith of Jews in the Western world, particularly America. Obviously no one person can do justice to this theme. The author's personal views must inevitably affect his selections and evaluations. Nevertheless, this writer, aware of the need, will attempt with maximum possible objectivity to delineate for thoughtful Jews and non-Jews the common essentials of current Jewish beliefs and practices.

Although this is designed as a positive statement of living Judaism, cognizance is taken also of the desire to learn the differences between Christianity and Judaism. Comparisons will be made for the purpose of clarification, not to assert superiority. An ancient rabbi said, "There is a place in God's kingdom for the righteous of all nations." It is this rabbi's view also.

3

If Christians were asked about their beliefs, most of them could refer to authoritative catechisms, creeds and confessions. But the Jew has no such answer to give. For there is no creed which all Jews accept. Although associations of synagogues exist for practical purposes, there is no supreme ecclesiastical body with authority over the souls of Jews. Nor are there priests to dispense grace, absolution, unction. The whole concept of salvation as redemption from sin in this world and from its consequences in the hereafter is alien to the main trends of Jewish thought. Religion for the Jew is primarily, though not entirely, a way of life here and now. It is a special kind of life, God-centered and ethically motivated. Its chief reward is the good life itself. Most Jews have assented to the judgment of an olden rabbinic teacher who, after describing our earthly life as an antechamber, added, "One hour of repentance and good deeds in this world is better than the whole life of the world to come."

By its very nature, Judaism has permitted diversity of practice and latitude of belief. Yet a great common denominator of faith has united Jews through the centuries and today characterizes most American Jews. This unique agreement is not imposed from the top down but wells up from the depth of the Jewish heart, nourished from hallowed traditions.

In the days of ancient Israel, the priesthood at Jerusalem was the accepted spiritual authority. Then in 586 B.C. Nebuchadnezzar besieged Jerusalem, demol-

4

ished Solomon's Temple and carried the Jews into exile in Babylon. With their Temple and their priesthood gone, the Jews found themselves in strange new communities where they formed voluntary assemblages for common worship and study of the law. These congregations were called synagogues. This institution proved so valuable that it has been continued to this day. It also provided the basic pattern for the churches which, after Paul, the Christians set up and developed along more unified lines. Among the Jews, however, the synagogue has survived in its pristine form. Any ten adult male Jews today can establish a congregation.

The congregation's rabbi is a teacher, not a priest. He has no ecclesiastical authority except as an expounder of the law. In fact, he is not even necessary to the functioning of the synagogue. Any male Jew with sufficient knowledge of the prayers and the laws can conduct a religious service. He may also officiate at marriages and bury the dead. During World War II, although more than half the rabbis of the country volunteered for the chaplaincy, and 311 actually served in uniform, they could not begin to cover the multitudinous units in which Jews were found. Consequently, on many of the battlefronts of Europe and on the remote Pacific islands, Jewish officers and enlisted personnel officiated at religious services.

In former times the rabbi was not even expected to earn his living by the law. Some of the most famous scholars were by trade cobblers and smiths. It was the

5

secularization of Jewish life in modern times which made a professional rabbinate essential. Now the layman has little time for study; learning is concentrated in the person of the rabbi. A student is ordained to the rabbinate only after a most rigorous course of study. The principal American seminaries require a minimum of four years of concentrated Judaic studies beyond college graduation. As a result of a careful process of selection and prolonged study, the rabbis are, as a rule, men of learning and culture, qualified for spiritual leadership. But they are not priests. They administer no sacraments. They do not lay down the law; at best they interpret it.

In the unbreakable fortress of Jewish spirituality the Torah is the repository for the Law of Judaism. Torah has a triple meaning. Primarily it is the sacred scrolls to be found in every synagogue. These are contained in an ark which is either built into the eastern wall of the structure, or protrudes from it as a chest. Although Judaism prohibits "graven images," the ark is exquisitely ornamental. It is an abiding reminder of the biblical Ark of the Covenant in which the Tablets of the Law were carried. Traditionally the ark is placed on that wall which, when faced by the worshipers, would direct their gaze and thoughts toward Jerusalem. In the ark the Torah scrolls are deposited. These are written by hand on parchment. The workmanship is fastidious and often beautiful, the product of painstaking effort on the part of one who is usually a descendant of generations of scribes. The mistake of a letter will make the scroll unusable. In 1908 when the synagogue of which this writer is now minister burned down, an Irish policeman dashed to the ark and seized the Torah. He handed it to the rabbi who was rushing up to the building. "Here," he said, "I saved your crucifix." Well, the Jews have no crucifix, but the policeman had the right idea; the scrolls are the most sacred symbols of Judaism.

Second, Torah means the Pentateuch—the first five books of the Bible—Genesis, Exodus, Leviticus, Numbers, Deuteronomy. These books are the acknowledged foundation of Judaism. They contain the principles of the faith, the Ten Commandments, the laws of holiness. The Pentateuch is the biography of the greatest Jew of all time, Moses. It describes the formation of the Jewish nation and the development of its faith. It runs the whole gamut of Jewish spiritual experience from the sublime poetry of the creation narrative to the minutiae of hygienic laws. So precious is the Pentateuch to the Jews that they divide it into fixed weekly portions and read them on every Sabbath in the year with special readings on holy days. And when the sacred round is completed, there is the gay festival of Simchas Torah, rejoicing in the law, at which the last verses of Deuteronomy are followed by the first verses of Genesis, symbolizing the eternal cycle of the law.

Finally, Torah means teaching, learning, doctrine. If a Jew says, "Let us study Torah," he might be referring

to the Pentateuch or to the Prophets or to the Talmud
or any of the sacred writings. He is certainly referring
to the first obligation of the Jew which is the study of
God's ways and requirements as revealed in holy writ.

The educational process for a Jew begins not later
than the age of five. According to tradition, a drop of
honey is placed on the first page the child is to learn
to read; he kisses it, thus beginning an association of
pleasantness which is expected to last through life.
When most of the world was illiterate, every Jewish boy
could read and by thirteen was advanced in the study of
a complex literature. Thus arose the love of learning,
the keenness of intellect, to be found among so many
Jews, even among those who have rejected the milieu
that made them what they are.

Although Jews love learning for its own sake, their
primary interest is the study of the law. To the religious
Jew the Torah is no burdensome legalism. It is an un-
ending source of inspiration, wisdom and practical help.
Its requirements bring God into his life every day, constantly. He begins and ends the day with prayers. He
thanks God before and after every meal, even when he
washes his hands. All his waking day the traditional
Jew wears a ritual scarf beneath his outer garments
which reminds him of God's nearness and love. There
are prescribed prayers for childbirth, circumcision,
marriage, illness, death. Even the appearance of a rain-
bow evokes an ancient psalm of praise. In effect, law
means the sanctification of all of life.

8

Jews never regarded the codification of law as a strait jacket. One basic device keeps it fluid. There is not only the written law, but also the oral law. The former is fixed; the latter was subject to emendation, interpretation, adaptation. For example, the ancient Torah says, "An eye for an eye." In itself this was an advance over the laws of the surrounding tribes which usually prescribed death for the taking of an eye. There is no Jewish record to indicate that the *lex talionis* was ever applied, or even intended, literally. Nevertheless the sages were not content to let this law remain ambiguous. They said that the intent of the law was to compel the offender to pay in damages the accepted equivalent for the loss of an eye. Thus the original phraseology was not repudiated but became the basis of a sensible adaptation to the realities of human society. As another example, the Torah proclaimed, "Remember the Sabbath day to keep it holy." Jews observed this commandment with the greatest seriousness. But life made its demands which could not be denied. So, in the oral law the rabbis evolved a whole series of exceptions. They said the Sabbath could be violated to bring help to the sick or to defend oneself against attack. They formulated it into the principle that the Sabbath was made for man, not man for the Sabbath.

The Lord Is One

𝒯HE central prayer of Judaism is the Shema: "Hear O Israel, the Lord our God, the Lord is One." This is the heart of every Jewish service. More, it is recited by the Jew when he believes death is approaching. Together with, "Thou shalt love the Lord thy God with all thy heart," it is to be found in printed form in the Mezuzah, the little tubed case placed on the doorposts of the homes of observant Jews, a constant reminder of God's presence and a sign of the Jewishness of the inhabitants.

The Shema and its correlative ideal, "Thou shalt love thy neighbor as thyself," originated in antiquity. They are found first in the books of Leviticus and Deuteronomy. Originally this affirmation of God's unity was a protest against idolatry. An ancient Jewish legend relates that the boy, Abraham, was left in charge of the idol shop when his father was off on business. He smashed every idol except the largest in whose hands he placed a club. The father, on returning, raged with disbelief when the son insisted that the big statue had destroyed the others. "How can it be?" demanded Terah. "These idols cannot think or do anything." "Let your ears hear what your mouth is declaring," said the boy who was destined to become the father of the Jewish people. In his quest for the true God, Abraham first worshiped the sun. When it went down, he knew it could not be the ever-present ruler. The moon, the stars, the seasons won his admiration but he soon realized that they were only handmaidens of the Most High, manifestations of the One who ruled over all. The entire history of the Hebrews in Palestine is marked by the struggles between the prophets who spoke for the one God and the backsliding people who preferred visible idols to the invisible Jehovah. Among the Jewish people the battle was won ultimately by the affirmers of God's unity. Paganism, however, continues in the world, and every new manifestation, including the deification of the state in our own time, rouses the Jew to reaffirm his faith in the one and only God of the world.

Following Paul, the Shema took on a new significance. Although Jews are able to understand Jesus, the Jew of Nazareth, they have never been able to understand or accept the idea of the Trinity. Down through the ages innumerable Jews suffered and many were put to death for rejecting this church doctrine. Invariably their last breath reaffirmed their faith in God's unity. Thus from the beginning of the Christian era to this very day, the Shema has been the rallying point of Jew-

12

ish loyalty confronting the persecution or the blandishments of the daughter religion.

For the modern American Jew two meanings have emerged which, while not new, are current in their emphasis. The first is suggested by Albert Einstein who, although not observant of formal religion, is profoundly Jewish in his religious outlook. More than any other living man, he has demonstrated the unity which binds the atom to the stars. According to his theories, God's world is indeed one, and wonderful. He writes, "I believe in Spinoza's God who reveals Himself in the orderly harmony of what exists. . . . It is enough for me to contemplate the mystery of conscious life perpetuating itself through all eternity, to reflect upon the marvelous structure of the universe which we dimly perceive, and to try humbly to comprehend even an infinitesimal part of the intelligence manifested in nature." This is a Jewish scientist's affirmation of God's unity. And Judaism accepts it. For, although the tradition is inflexible in its insistence on the existence of God, it is broadly tolerant of varying God concepts. Its catholicity embraces them all, from the religion of Einstein which he says is, ". . . the feeling from which true scientific research draws its spiritual sustenance" to the piety of the simple Jewish shepherd who prayed, "Lord of the Universe, it is apparent and known to You that if You had cattle and gave them to me to tend, though I take wages for tending all others, from You I would take nothing, for I love You."

13

From God to man, from His Fatherhood to our brotherhood, this is the second meaning of the Shema to modern Jews. The concept of human oneness has always been an integral element in the Jewish religious outlook. Frequently this has been misunderstood because of the Jews' insistence on remaining a distinctive group. The Jew has never believed that brotherhood means regimentation, the elimination of differences, the overcoming of minorities by dominant majorities. Loving your neighbor as yourself, he believes, requires respect for differences. The test of maturity in personal and group relations is the capacity to accept differences and to employ them fruitfully. The very prophet who insisted on Israel's unique mission went on to say, "Have we not all one Father? Did not one God make us all?" Another prophet proclaimed that the Ethiopians were as precious to God as the Jews. One of the greatest rabbis who lived over two thousand years ago said that the most important statement in the Bible was not the Ten Commandments but, "This is the book of the generations of man." To the Jews themselves the scriptures were not the heritage of a single people but of all humanity.

The prayer which after the Shema has the deepest hold on all Jews is the Kaddish. In actual practice it is the prayer honoring the dead. It is recited for a year after the death of a loved one and on the anniversaries thereafter. It is also read in every Jewish service because of its historical meaning. The Kaddish in exact

14

translation contains no reference to the dead. Its solemn phrases exalt the name of God and pray for the coming of His kingdom. "Exalted and hallowed be the name of God throughout the world. . . . May His kingdom come, His will be done." There is no doubt that Jesus spoke this ancient prayer in the synagogue and that it became the basis for the Lord's Prayer.

Originally the Kaddish was a hymn of praise to the Almighty, and was recited at the close of religious exercises and sessions of study. Then, because of its associations, it was chanted when great scholars and leaders died. Subsequently, the democratic outlook of Judaism asserted itself and insisted that the Kaddish be included in the final service for all who had been translated to the "Academy on High." The Kaddish, though honoring the dead, does not make specific the Jewish attitude toward immortality. Perhaps this is because the Jews have never agreed on what happens after death. Most Jews of recent centuries have recited the Credo of Maimonides, the twelfth-century physician-philosopher who affirmed the physical resurrection of the dead. But the hearts of many stricken Jews have also echoed the lament of Job, "As the cloud is consumed and vanisheth away so he that goeth down to the grave shall come up no more." It is growing harder for modern Jews to believe in physical resurrection. This probably accounts for the increasing trend toward cremation which is found among non-Orthodox Jews. Among American Jews, the Kaddish is returning more

15

to its original meaning, the acknowledgment of God's rule and the readiness to leave our ultimate fate in His hands. This finds poignant expression in the prayer recited before the Kaddish in the Reform service:

All you who mourn the loss of loved ones, and, at this hour, remember the sweet companionship and the cherished hopes that have passed away with them, give ear to the word of comfort spoken in the name of God. Only the body has died and has been laid in the dust. The spirit lives in the shelter of God's love and mercy. Our loved ones continue, also, in the remembrance of those to whom they were precious. Their deeds of loving kindness, the true and beautiful words they spoke are treasured up as incentives to conduct by which the living honor the dead. And when we ask in our grief: Whence shall come our help and our comfort? then in the strength of faith let us answer with the Psalmist: My help cometh from God. He will not forsake us nor leave us in our grief. Upon Him we cast our burden and He will grant us strength according to the days He has apportioned to us. All life comes from Him; all souls are in His keeping. Come then, and in the midst of sympathizing fellow-worshipers, rise and hallow the name of God.

The Jewish Year

*T*HE catechism of the Jew is his calendar," said Samson Raphael Hirsch, nineteenth-century German rabbi. One can learn more about the mainsprings of the Jew's spirituality from the cycle of year-round observances than from any formal statement of faith. In these are revealed his habits of thought and feeling, the historic memories he chooses to keep alive, as well as the functioning patterns of his religious conduct. Reference here is not to the actual monthly calendar with all its irregularities. In the Jewish year, the lunar cycle is twenty-nine and one-half days which determines the length of the month. Thus one month is twenty-nine days and the next month is thirty days. Normally then, twelve months add up to 353 or 355 days. Seven times in a cycle of nineteen years, an extra month is added to the year to compensate for the extra days of the solar year. Thus, in 1949, the new year began on September 24—in 1950, September 12—in 1951, October 1.

It is the annual cycle of Jewish religious observances to which we are referring. Traditionally, the most significant of these has been the Sabbath which begins with dusk on Friday evening and continues until sunset on Saturday. Its great importance can be deduced from its place in the Ten Commandments. No other holy day observance is included in this listing of the basic requirements of Judaism. A careful reading of the Fourth Commandment will suggest the reasons for including Sabbath observance among the great affirmations and prohibitions of the Jewish faith:

"Observe the Sabbath day, to keep it holy, as the Lord thy God commanded thee. Six days shalt thou labour, and do all thy work; but the seventh day is a Sabbath unto the Lord thy God, in it thou shalt not do any manner of work, thou, nor thy son, nor thy daughter, nor thy manservant, nor thy maidservant, nor thine ox, nor thine ass, nor any of thy cattle, nor thy stranger that is within thy gates; that thy manservant and thy maidservant may rest as well as thou. And thou shalt remember that thou wast a servant in the land of Egypt, and the Lord thy God brought thee out thence by a mighty hand and by an outstretched arm; therefore the Lord thy God commanded thee to keep the Sabbath day."

The most obvious reason for resting every seventh day is humanitarian. Some writers maintain that this is the most important contribution ever made to the working people of the world. The ancient Hebrews lived among empires in which the ruling classes enjoyed leisurely, elegant lives and the masses worked incessantly. Professing a religion which affirmed that all men were created in the image of God, they abhorred slavery. Their social consciousness transformed ancient Eastern taboo days related to cycles of the moon into a fixed weekly day of rest. But not for themselves alone. Remembering their own bondage in Egypt, they wanted their manservants and maidservants to enjoy the respite as well. In a world more profoundly plagued by xenophobia than our own, they insisted that the stranger was also entitled to equal benefits. Nor humans alone either. Their animals, too, were not to be worked on the Sabbath day.

The Roman Seneca ridiculed the Jews for wasting every seventh day in idleness. However, they were not only more humane but also wiser than he was. They had anticipated the findings of modern efficiency engineers. Regular rest and recreation enable men to work better, to produce more. The Sabbath undoubtedly helped Jews to become an energetic, industrious and creative people. The common sense of the Sabbath and its humaneness commended themselves to the daughter religions of Judaism. Although Christianity and Mohammedanism rejected many Jewish concepts, they retained the institution of the Sabbath, a fixed day each week for rest and worship. Thus an ancient covenant hewn from the social consciousness of a little desert tribe

19

became in time an established practice for the entire civilized world.

However, we underestimate the significance of the Sabbath if we think of it principally in terms of social welfare. As with most Jewish institutions, there is an inextricable commingling of humanitarian concern and religious faith. This is to be seen in the other version of the Fourth Commandment which appears in the twentieth chapter of the Book of Exodus:

In six days the Lord made the heaven and earth and sea and all that in them is, and rested on the seventh day: wherefore the Lord blessed the Sabbath day, and hallowed it.

Both the Orthodox Jew who accepts this statement literally and the liberal who acknowledges its spiritual truth regard the Sabbath as holy. It set Jews apart as a distinct group committed to worship God in their own way. This was understood by those who have sought to destroy Judaism. Roman emperors forbade the observance of the Sabbath. The Soviet Government in its war on religion has rotated the day of rest making it impossible for all Jews, or all Christians, to observe the Sabbath at the same time.

Yes, the Jews and their enemies have understood that the Sabbath is essential to the preservation of Judaism. Jewish home life revolves around it. The Sabbath eve nourishes the beauties, the tendernesses, the poetry and the strengths of Jewish family life. It turns the hearts of the parents to the children, and the children to the parents. It inspires memories which bless Jews in adversity and console them in sorrow. It sings its way into their hearts. Even physically it helped to sustain the Jews. For no matter how poorly they lived during the week, on the Sabbath, through their own efforts or communal aid, they ate well.

To the traditional Jew the Sabbath has presented some restrictive features. Nothing might be done which would constitute a breach of the command to rest. Ordinary weekday activities must be set aside on the hallowed seventh day. There were hardships involved in not lighting the fires, not cooking, not riding, not carrying objects, including money. But Jewish common sense forbade extremism in such matters. These regulations could be set aside for reasons of health, safety or self-defense. In the Book of Maccabees it is related that the priest, Mattathias, permitted the Jews to take up arms on the Sabbath to protect their homes and their faith. The Mishnah rules that a burning lamp may be extinguished on the Sabbath for fear of robbers, but never to save fuel. If a difference of opinion arose among physicians at a patient's bedside, the law favored him who recommended violation of the Sabbath to save the patient's life.

To compensate for its restrictions the Sabbath offered special delights. No unpleasantness was permitted on this day. Funerals were prohibited; even mourning was forbidden. Except for Yom Kippur, the Sabbath of Sabbaths, Jews were required to eat on the Sabbath

21

even when a fast day fell on it. Its music had a special sweetness; its prayers had a flavor of their own.

For this writer, the Sabbath evokes many memories —of his sainted mother blessing the Sabbath candles; of the fresh warm *challah,* the twisted Sabbath bread; of the filled fish, a foretaste of Leviathan; of the melodic "Lecho Dodi" in the synagogue, the welcome of the Sabbath bride; of the cantor's flourishes over the sanctification of the wine; of the friendly *"Good Shabbos"* as all hurried from the synagogue to the Sabbath table at home.

And more recent memories . . . of the Gerer Rebbi, the famous Polish mystic who in 1925 asked only one question of a young Reform rabbi, "Do you observe the Sabbath?" . . . of Samuel Reshevsky, the chess champion who, desiring to eat in an Orthodox home during a chess tournament in Rochester, set up a single test, "Do they observe the Sabbath?" . . . of a Shavuos memorial service in the displaced persons' camp in Feldafing, Germany, in 1946 where nearly every worshiper grieved for the loss of most of his family. The rabbi, himself a mourner, offered no easy consolations. Out of the immemorial wisdom of his people, he urged them to observe the Sabbath, for this was the Jewish way to healing and strength.

Holy Days

Holy Days

Abraham, says the Book of Genesis, was asked by the Lord to sacrifice his only son. But at the last moment the Lord let him substitute a ram. Today the blowing of the shofar, or ram's horn, which celebrates Abraham's act of extreme devotion to his God, highlights the service for Rosh Hashonah, or New Year, and signals the end of Yom Kippur, the Day of Atonement.

*T*HE Jewish new year begins in the early fall. Its observances are far removed in spirit from the celebrations surrounding January 1, for it ushers in a ten-day period of penitence culminating in the fast of Yom Kippur. The new year is regarded not as the occasion for carousing but for spiritual stock-taking. What is man? What is our life? What will be our fate? Some Jews have believed literally, others metaphorically, that on the new year the books of life are spread open before the Great Judge. In this period of judgment it is determined, "Who shall live and who shall die, who shall be at rest and who shall wander, who shall be tranquil and who shall be harassed, who shall become poor and who shall wax rich, who shall be brought low and who shall be exalted."

There is, in this holy day period, a very solemn approach to the facts of our frail human existence. No attempt is made to gloss over the evils of life. God's ways may be inscrutable but ultimately they are accepted as just. Therefore, the fear of the Lord is the beginning of wisdom. Judaism offers no easy way to God. No son has been sent down to take us by the hand and lead us to Him. No mediator intercedes for us. No priest dispenses God's grace. In the final accounting, there is a purely personal relationship between the individual and his God. This is an awesome responsibility. Need we wonder then that this penitential period is known as The Days of Awe? Even the blowing of the shofar, the ram's horn, which from Biblical times has announced the new year, penetrates into the heart of the modern Jew and causes it to tremble.

The climax is reached on Yom Kippur. Like all Jewish holidays it begins at sundown, for Jews follow the biblical pattern of creation—"There was evening and there was morning, one day." The service opens with the Kol Nidre chant. This is the most stirring, the most haunting melody in the entire religious experience of Jews. The words of the song are hardly relevant to present conditions. They constitute a plea for release from vows which cannot be kept, and refer to religious commitments, not promises between man and man. In the period of forced conversions of Jews to Christianity, this prayer for absolution came to be associated with vows made under duress. Today when Jews hear the Kol Nidre they think of the centuries of persecution

26

and of the six million who were slaughtered by the Nazis, and they are bound by mystic ties to their ancestors and to their living brethren throughout the world.

After the evening service, some Jews remain in the synagogue all night and stay on until the services conclude at sundown the next day. Most American Jews, however, go back to their homes after the evening prayers and return the next morning to remain for the entire day. They fast for twenty-four hours, fulfilling an ancient injunction. This reminds them of their human frailty and of their dependence on God. It establishes the necessary mood of self-discipline and of self-sacrifice.

The spiritual concern of Yom Kippur is with our human sinfulness, but what is sin? To answer this question we must go back to Judaism's balanced interpretation of the nature of man. On the one hand there are no perfect saints in the Jewish tradition. Even Moses, the greatest Jew of all time, was denied admittance to the promised land because he disobeyed God. Jacob in the earlier stages of his life was selfish and crafty, yet his name was changed to Israel and he became the progenitor of his people. It is significant that after he wrestled with the angel he limped; no one achieves complete victory over our human weaknesses.

Judaism, on the other hand, does not regard man as inherently sinful or depraved. Our instinctual drives are considered good because God gave them to us. Marriage is not regarded as merely "better than burning" with desire, a sort of limited concession to man's wicked nature, but as the fulfillment of the wondrous senses that God has given us. So asceticism is rare in Judaism. There are no hermits, no retreats to monasteries. Celibacy is not required of the rabbis. Not merely human needs but Divine Law, says the medieval poet, Gabirol, insists that we give every faculty its due. One of the noblest ethical documents of all Jewish literature, eleventh-century's Bachya's, "Duties of the Heart" states, "On the Day of Judgment, a man will be called to account for every innocent pleasure and enjoyment he has denied himself." The rabbis of the Talmud maintain that much good has come from our so-called "evil desires." They say that our sex drive has produced love, marriage, the family, the perpetuation of the race. Without the acquisitive instinct, they claim, homes would not be built, fields would not be tilled. Therefore, in the "Ethics of the Fathers," a beloved rabbi asks, "If I am not for myself, who will be for me, but if I am for myself alone, what am I?" Always the balance, always the confronting of man's weaknesses with his potentialities, always the practical instruments for living the good life, for returning to God.

In its Hebrew origin the most commonly used word for sin actually means "missing the mark." It is the denial of the heritage, the repudiation of God's commandments. There are, it must be added, various formula-

28

tions of God's requirements. The Torah, the basic law contained in the Pentateuch, lists six hundred and thirteen commands ranging from dietary specifications to right motivations. ("Thou shalt not covet.") Micah reduced them to three, "To do justly, to love mercy and to walk humbly before God." How do we walk in God's ways? The answer is given in the climactic moment of the Yom Kippur morning service when the rabbi stands before the open ark about to remove the sacred scrolls. He prays in the words proclaimed of old to Moses, "God, merciful, gracious, long-suffering, abundant in goodness and ever true." Such are God's ways; such must be ours. Note the constant emphasis on mercy. This led the late Chief Rabbi Hertz to conclude that in Judaism the chief sin is callousness to the suffering of any of God's creatures. Consequently, atonement must include not only *rapprochement* with God but also expiation toward our fellowmen. The evil decree, says the tradition, is averted by prayer, penitence and acts of loving-kindness.

Judaism is insistent on the last of these as an indispensable requirement for atonement. On Yom Kippur God forgives our sins against Him but not the wrongs we have done our fellowmen. Acts of penitential restitution can alone clear the way for God's grace. The rabbis go beyond this and say, "Whoever has a sin to confess and is ashamed to do so, let him go and do a good deed and he will find forgiveness." *Gemilas Chasodim*

—acts of loving-kindness—are associated not only with Yom Kippur but with almost every major Jewish holiday. Before Passover, Jews contribute to *Maos Chittim*, the fund to provide for the holiday needs of poor families. In the Passover ritual the head of the household lifts the unleavened bread and recites, "This is the bread of affliction which our fathers ate in the land of Egypt. Let all who are hungry come and eat. Let all who are in need come and celebrate with us." On Chanukah and Purim, gifts are given especially to the poor. The offerings of fruits and flowers brought by children for Succos are distributed to the sick and needy. Significantly, the Hebrew word for charity is *tzedokah* which literally means righteousness. Charitableness is not optional; it is an absolute requirement of Judaism. Jews may differ about the methods or beneficiaries of specific philanthropies. They may argue about the amounts they are expected to give. The late Rabbi Wise once said that you cannot get two Jews to agree about anything except what a third Jew should give to charity. But all Jews are in substantial agreement about their obligations to charitableness.

This deep impulse, these strong habits cultivated through the generations have been a major factor in building the structure of Jewish philanthropy. Its foundation has been a sense of communal responsibility for the needy. Maimonides' "Eight Degrees of Charity," written nearly eight centuries ago, reflected the accepted Jewish standards of charitableness:

1. Those who bestow charity but with grumbling.
2. Those who do so cheerfully but give less than they ought.
3. Those who contribute only when they are asked and what they are asked.
4. Those who give before they are requested to do so.
5. Those who give charity but do not know who benefits by it, although the recipient is aware from whom he has received it.
6. Those who give charity and do not disclose their names to those who received it.
7. Those who do not know to whom their contribution will be given while the recipients do not know from whom they have received it.
8. Those who extend a loan or bestow a gift upon the needy, or who take a poor man into partnership or help him to establish himself in business so that he should not be compelled to apply for charity. Such people practice the highest degree of charity.

The tradition expected each Jew to give from a tenth to a fifth of his income to charity. This ratio was exceeded in the sacrificial generosity summoned to save the survivors of the Nazi onslaught. In the year 1948, for example, the United Jewish Appeal raised $150,-000,000 from the American Jewish community of 5,000,000 persons. Compare this with the $72,000,000 raised by the American Red Cross in the same year from the total American population of nearly 150,000,-

31

000, to which Jews also contributed their share, to be made aware of the tremendous role which sympathy and charitableness play in the Jewish outlook.

The humanitarian requirements of atonement are summed up in the verses from Isaiah which are read in the Yom Kippur morning service. Lest worshipers get the notion that their prayers of penitence are sufficient, they are reminded,

Is not this the fast that I have chosen?
To loose the fetters of wickedness,
To undo the bands of the yoke,
And to let the oppressed go free. . . .
Is it not to deal thy bread to the hungry
And that thou bring the homeless to thy house?
When thou seest the naked, that thou cover him,
And that thou hide not thyself from thy fellow man.
Then shall thy light break forth as the morning . . .
And thy righteousness shall go before thee.

Loving-kindness, however, is not sufficient. Judaism sponsors no atheistic humanitarianism. Man was created by God and endowed with high potentialities. If he has denied his heritage, he must find his way back to God. The underlying assumption in this quest is that he has free will. Jews, like other religionists, have been troubled by the paradox of man's sinfulness. Why, if we were created by a good and omnipotent God, do we have and use the capacity to do evil? Judaism has no general theological explanation of "sin" such as Chris-

tianity offers in the doctrine of man's fall. Committing
a sin is, in the Jewish religion, not something for which
man is destined because it is his preordained fate. Sin-
ning is something the individual may or may not do,
depending upon his character. The rabbis say that
everything is in the hands of God but the fear of God.
The color, the sex, the physical structure of the unborn
child are predetermined, but not whether he will do
right or wrong.

To men and women, then, with freedom of choice
comes the great challenge of the Yom Kippur service:

"Behold, I set before thee this day life and good, and
death and evil . . . therefore choose life that ye may
live."

In the atonement process there is a profound mystical
element. God meets us halfway. First, we must acknowl-
edge our waywardness. He who recognizes his sin has
already begun to loosen its hold on him. Then, where
possible, there must be expiation, restitution. Now the
Jew is ready for penitent prayer. His supplications are
personal, yet also communal. Many of them are in the
plural form, "*We* have sinned, *we* have done perverse-
ly." Thus it is recognized how deeply we are involved in
one another's weaknesses and failures. Then, worn with
fasting, humble in penitence, the worshiper may be
ready for God's forgiveness. But God's forgiveness does
not come easy. He searches the innermost recesses of
the heart; no secrets are hidden from Him. His prob-

33

ings make His task of forgiveness even more difficult. So on Yom Kippur, say the rabbis, even God Himself prays:

> May my mercy conquer my wrath
> So that I may treat my children with love.

Succos

Historically the Festival of Tabernacles is associated with harvest time and prayers of thanksgiving. Because it also is connected with the Exodus, when the Jews were forced to live in booths, today's Jew observes the occasion in a Succah, *or booth, adorned with fruit and with a roof open to God.*

$\mathcal{T}$HUS the fall holy days come to an end. They have been directed toward the individual. They have helped him search his own heart and better his own conduct. At once, as if to preserve the sense of balance, the other aspects of Judaism assert themselves. On the fifth day after Yom Kippur, the Festival of Tabernacles begins. Although its origins are not altogether clear, the holiday has been associated for millennia with two principal ideas. First, it is a reminder that the ancient Hebrews fleeing in the wilderness lived in frail shelters. Hence their descendants are expected every fall to erect temporary booths (*succos*) as a remembrance of their forefathers' hardships and spiritual triumphs. The *succah* is decorated with fruits, vegetables, branches, flowers, testimony to the bounty of the Creator. This leads to the second historic concept—thanksgiving. It is captured in a psalm of praise associated with the festival service, "O give thanks unto the Lord for He is good; His kindness endureth forever."

Here then are two basic Jewish attitudes. Unlike most other peoples with long and dramatic histories, the Jews stress the humbleness, not the glory, of their beginnings. In the great spring festival of freedom the celebrants are cautioned to remember, "Ye were slaves in the land of Egypt." No offspring of the gods, no heroes suckled by a wolf, Jews are never to forget that their history began in slavery. Succos serves a similar purpose by recalling with colorful symbolism our former low estate, the uncertainty of life, the unsureness of houses built by man's hand and finally our dependence on God.

Of course there is an element of pride in this emphasis on humility. Only a people with unshakeable faith in itself could survive such hardships. More than half a century ago Disraeli prophetically wrote, "The vineyards of Israel have ceased to exist. But the eternal law enjoins the children of Israel still to celebrate the vintage. A race that persists in celebrating their vintage, although they have no fruits to gather, will regain their vineyards."

This confidence flowed from their faith in God. It was not their merits which freed them from slavery and sustained them through the wilderness but God's mercy. Their gratitude was reinforced by the circumstances surrounding Succos. In the early fall all nature smiles. The grapes are ripe upon the vines; the trees are heavy with luscious fruit; the fields are gay with golden grain. The Jews loved nature but were no nature worshipers. It was not the creation but the Creator that evoked their praise. This conviction that a good God had made a good world was suggested in the very first chapter of the Bible, "And God saw everything that He had made, and, behold, it was very good." Even the hardships of Jewish history could not shake this faith.

Not that Jews did not have their differences with God. Abraham, learning that the good people of Sodom were to be destroyed with the wicked, cried out, "Shall not the Judge of all the earth do justice?" Even God Himself could be held accountable. But this was a lover's quarrel with the universe. Jews never doubted the existence of God although they sometimes questioned His ways. He was the source of all, the goal of all. Thus Jews were enjoined to leave an opening in the roof of the *succah* that the stars might be a visible reminder of God's presence and care.

In this spirit Succos is associated with the universalistic aspects of Judaism. The bliblical command to rejoice in the festival adds, "Thou, and thy son . . . and thy servant . . . and the stranger, and the fatherless, and the widow that are within thy gates." It was on Succos, according to the tradition, that the Temple of Solomon was dedicated. The King prayed not only for his own people but also "concerning the stranger that is not of thy people Israel . . . Hear Thou in heaven

Thy dwelling place, and do according to all the stranger asketh of Thee."

When, following an ancient custom, the bound branches of willow, myrtle and palm are waved in all directions, it is to indicate the universality of God's reign. The scriptural reading for Succos goes beyond this. It foretells the day when "the Lord shall be King over all the earth," when all nations will go up to Jerusalem, "to worship the Lord of Hosts and to observe the Festival of Tabernacles." The final thought is provided by a rabbi of the Talmudic period. He prophesied that in the world to come, when all other sacrifices will have ceased, the sacrifice of thanksgiving shall endure forever and ever.

Only under one condition were prayers of thanksgiving not to be uttered—over the suffering of others. According to the rabbis of the Midrash, God Himself set this pattern when He was compelled to rebuke His own ministering angels for rejoicing over the death of the pursuing Egyptians. He silenced them: "My children are drowning and ye sing praises unto Me!" In the same spirit the tradition decrees that no blessing may be pronounced over an act of charity. Jews were expected to recite a *berochoh*, a prayer praising God, over most of life's experiences. Why not over a charitable deed? "Because," said the rabbinic fathers, "one does not thank God for another's misfortune even though it provide the occasion for generous conduct."

The deeper meaning of this ancient, lovely festival,

its mood of thankfulness, of tempered joy, humility, wonder, abounding faith, are caught up in the beautiful prayer at the heart of the Succos service:

Every living soul shall praise Thee; the spirit of all flesh shall glorify Thy name. Thou art God from everlasting to everlasting and besides Thee there is no redeemer nor savior. Thou art the first and the last, the Lord of all generations. Thou rulest the world in kindness and all Thy creatures in mercy. Thou art our guardian who sleepeth not and slumbereth not. To Thee alone we give thanks. Yet, though our lips should overflow with song, and our tongues with joyous praise, we should still be unable to thank Thee even for a thousandth part of the bounties which Thou hast bestowed upon our fathers and upon us. Thou hast been our protector and our savior in every trial and peril. Thy mercy has watched over us, and Thy loving-kindness has never failed us.

The Kotzker Rebbi said that joyfulness is the outcome of holiness. This is a valid conclusion covering the religious life of Jews through the centuries. It also correctly describes the cycle of Jewish fall holidays. From the solemnity of Rosh Hashonah to the soul searching of Yom Kippur to the thankfulness of Succos to the rejoicing of Simchas Torah—these are the steps from holiness to joy.

One can learn much about the soul of a people from the things it rejoices in. Some nations rejoice in their power; others in military conquests; others in their artists and singers. The Nazis, according to the survivors of the concentration camps, derived exquisite joy from cruelty.

The Jews traditionally have rejoiced in the law. About the tenth century, Simchas Torah was attached to the Succos holiday, an appropriate conclusion. It became a day of spirited rejoicing. The scrolls were carried around the synagogue in gay processions. Revered rabbis, learned scholars, pious elders would throw their customary reserve to the winds and dance and sing. The womenfolk, ordinarily seated in the balconies, participate in the general jubilation and the children are served refreshments within the synagogue itself. All branches of Judaism have found some way to celebrate Simchas Torah in this spirit.

The celebration of Simchas Torah at the displaced persons' camp in Babenhausen, Germany, in 1946 will never be forgotten by the author. These uprooted Jews had just come to this grim camp. They had suffered for many years. They had been tortured in concentration camps. They had been driven from land to land before the Nazi fury. They were now homeless among the very people who had caused their misfortune. No solution of their problem was in sight. Nevertheless, at the service that morning, in a crudely improvised synagogue, they danced and sang with such joy as if they had been the beneficiaries of God's greatest bounty. In fact, they believed they were the beneficiaries of God's greatest bounty, namely, His law.

Chanukah

Chanukah

In the year 168 B. C., King Antiochus IV ordered the Jews to worship an idol he set up in the Temple of Jerusalem. The Jews revolted, drove the Syrians out and rededicated the Temple, burning a cruse of oil that lasted eight days. Today Jews mark the eight days by lighting eight candles.

*C*HANUKAH, which comes in December, is historical and deeply spiritual. It commemorates the Jewish nation's successful struggle against oppression by Antiochus IV. This Syrian ruler was one of those who inherited part of the empire of Alexander the Great. Zealous Hellenist and unifier, he sought to impose Greek ways on the people whom he ruled. Some of the Jews yielded to the blandishments of the pleasant Greek customs or to curry favor with the King. However, the Hebraic genius sensed the fatal danger in this process and expressed itself in a revolt of the common people. Led by Mattathias, an elderly priest in the town of Modin and later by his son, Judah the Maccabee, they strove to cast off the oppressive yoke. At first shouting, "Whosoever is zealous of the Law, let him follow me," Mattathias led the attack on Jews who were disloyal to their faith. Then Judah, apparently a military genius, organized his loyal followers into bands which carried on successful guerrilla operations against the foreign oppressors. The odds were against them for they were ill-equipped and vastly outnumbered. But they knew the hills and caves of Judea as the enemy did not. And they were fighting for their homes and their faith and their freedom as the Syrian mercenaries were not. As the months passed, as early defeats were transformed into victories, they demonstrated the historic validity of Zechariah's promise, "Not by might, not by power, but by My spirit, saith the Lord."

By the early winter of 165 B.C. they delivered the last decisive blows to the demoralized armies of Antiochus. Judah marched victoriously into Jerusalem. His first act was to cleanse the Temple of its polution. A single undefiled cruse of oil was found. It alone was used. For the law stipulated that only such vessels of oil whose seals were opened by authorized persons could be utilized for the sanctuary. Tradition has it that this single flask provided enough oil to burn not for one, but for eight days.

Ever since, the Jews have celebrated in the Hebrew month of Kislev, corresponding in a general way to the month of December, the festival of Chanukah—dedication. The Book of Maccabees is read. Special prayers of rejoicing are sung for the wonders God wrought for His people. Jewish homes are gladdened with eight nights of celebration and gift giving. Candles are lit, one the first night, two the second—until finally eight are kindled on the last night. There was an interesting dispute between the followers of Hillel and the disciples of Shammai over the order of the candles. The latter advocated the lighting of eight on the first night moving downward toward a single light on the last night. This may have reflected their basic view that the glory of Israel lay in the past, that there had been a steady downward trend among the Jews. The followers of the benign Hillel who had proclaimed the Golden Rule before Jesus, were much more hopeful about Jewish history. They foresaw a glorious future for Judaism. Therefore, symbolic of their faith and hope, they advocated a rising crescendo of light. The historic wisdom of the Jew supported their view and it prevailed.

A modern vindication of this hopefulness was seen by the author on the island of Saipan in December, 1943. There he saw Jews in United States uniforms gathered for the Chanukah service. The thermometer registered over one hundred; the candles could hardly remain erect long enough for the completion of the chaplain's prayers. Bombs were falling in the area; suicide-bent Japanese soldiers were dashing out of nearby caves hurling grenades. American planes were warming up for the dangerous mission to Tokyo. In the midst of this inferno, the Jewish G.I.'s were singing "Mo'oz Tzur, Rock of Ages," the Chanukah hymn. Unshakeable was the faith which it and they expressed:

45

Yours the message cheering
That the time is nearing
Which will see
All men free,
Tyrants disappearing.

The basic issue of the Maccabean struggle was religious freedom. The Jews fought for their right to worship their God in their own way. This struggle apparently is never completely won. We have learned this again in our generation. The Maccabees learned it also in theirs, for not long after the victory of 165, war broke out again. This time Judah was killed in battle. Soon the new colossus, Rome, bestrode the Middle East. The Hebrew state was crushed, not to rise again until May, 1948. But the flag of religious freedom had been raised, not to come down again. It is interesting to speculate on what this victory of the spirit has meant in human history. If Judaism had been destroyed in the second century before Jesus, would Christianity have come into the world, or Mohammedanism? Both were products of Judaism; both derived sustenance from the living Jewish people.

The Jews have understood that not only their survival as a people but their faith, the Jewish soul, was at stake. For this reason, perhaps, the Hallel, stirring psalm of praise, is chanted on Chanukah but not on Purim which commemorates also the deliverance of the people. The Gerer Rebbi, once renowned Chassidic leader of Eastern Jewry, thus explains the greater importance of Chanukah. "On Purim we were saved from the attempt to destroy the body of the Jew; but on Chanukah we were rescued from the decree that would have destroyed our soul."

Purim

Purim

Ahasuerus, King of Persia, did not know his wife Esther was a Jew. When Esther learned that Haman, the vizier, was planning to wipe out the Jews because of hatred for Mordecai, she risked death by going to her husband, admitting her identity and exposing Haman's plot. Haman was executed. Today children dance and swing noisemakers at Purim's gay celebration.

*N*EVERTHELESS, Purim plays an important role in the history of the Jews. There is some doubt as to whether the events narrated in the Book of Esther are historically correct. Is the King Xerxes who reigned over Persia from 405 to 465 B.C. the same Ahasuerus who ruled, according to the biblical account, over 127 provinces? No other historical record exists which describes this attempt to destroy the Jews, nor their successful resistance. Of course this does not prove the Book of Esther to be inaccurate but it leads many scholars to the conclusion that the story is to be regarded as an historical novel. Calling Mordecai its hero, a descendant of Saul, and Haman its villain, an offspring of the Amalekite ruler who tried to kill the Jewish king and was himself put to death by the prophet Samuel, seems to establish the allegoric char-

acter of the tale. *"Sic semper tyrannis"*; that is its final
judgment on all the oppressors of the Jews.

Whether based on historic facts or not, Purim has
been highly significant in Jewish life. Its description of
anti-Semitism was confirmed by Jewish experience
through the centuries. It is as modern as the latest rant-
ing of a Jew-baiter. What are Haman's grievances
against Mordecai? The proud Jew would not bow down
to him. Why? The rabbis of the Talmud say that Mordecai would have no right to jeopardize the safety of
his people by an act of personal pride. But they add,
Haman wore over his breast a small idol; to this Mordecai was justified in refusing obeisance.

The independent Jew, loyal to his own way of life,
refused to subordinate his values to the idol-worshiping
vizier. Haman got the point. He said to the King,
"There is a people in our midst whose ways are differ-
ent." Right. Then, in true anti-Semitic fashion, he continues, "They do not obey the King's laws." This of
course was false. The Jews had not refused to obey
Ahasuerus. In fact, it later developed that Mordecai had
endangered his life in thwarting the plans of assassins
who had plotted to kill the King. An ancient cryptic
rabbinic decree has defined the correct attitude of Jews
toward the laws of the country in which they live; *"Dinoh demalchusoh dinoh*—the law of the land is the
law."

Spiritually, however, the Jews have always insisted
on their right to obey the laws of their own Torah which

52

became, in time, the laws of their inmost being. Thus they could not worship idols of the Temple or of the State. They could not substitute a temporal ruler for the King of Kings. They would not violate the Sabbath for brutalizing sports or material gain. They loathed violence, at times accepting it reluctantly as a last resort, never good or glorious in itself. Regarding all men as God's children made in His image, they cherished human freedom and human dignity. Thus, most oppressors of man's free spirit have found the Jew not only irritating, even baffling, but also obstructionist. His independent mind, his humanitarian values, his moral courage and his unflagging loyalty to his invisible God stood as obstacles to regimentation and oppression.

Purim has another quality which made it popular. The Jews are essentially a serious people. They are not morbid, guilt-ridden, pessimistic. But from the beginning of their history they have taken a very realistic, hence serious, view of life. Duty ranks high in their scheme of values. "Thou shalt be holy for the Lord, thy God, is holy," does not allow for much nonsense. Nevertheless, possessing a rich sense of humor and needing release from life's tensions, they seized upon Purim as an occasion for gaiety and playfulness. Even the Book of Esther has an oriental, sensuous quality which is not typical of the Bible. It sounds rather like a tale from the *Arabian Nights*—the Queen Vashti who refused the King's request to disport herself before his guests and therefore was deposed; the beautiful unknown girl,

Esther, who was chosen Queen in her place (an Eastern version of the Cinderella story); the wicked plot against her people; the hero's intervention which saves the King's life in the nick of time; the exploitation of the Queen's beauty to reverse the evil decree; and finally the indignities and the gallows for the villain . . . what could be nicer? The very nature of the story encourages Jews to be gay on Purim. They enthusiastically follow the biblical pattern, "Therefore do the Jews make the fourteenth day of the month of Adar a day of gladness and feasting, a good day, and of sending gifts one to another."

Down through the centuries, despite their hardships, Jews have rejoiced with a kind of abandon on the winter's day chosen by the casting of lots (Purim). This gaiety was the more acceptable because Esther, unlike all the other books of the Bible, contains no mention of the name of God. So, even the synagogue becomes a house of mirth on Purim eve. Nefarious noisemakers are distributed among the children and used without restraint every time the reader of the Megillah (the Book of Esther) comes to Haman's name. The youngsters masquerade and present humorous plays. Gifts are exchanged. Special generosity toward the poor is customary, but even they are expected to give token gifts so their self-respect may be maintained.

Can we not understand then why the rabbis say that when all other holidays will have passed away, Jews will still be celebrating Purim?

Passover

Passover

When Pharoah refused to free the Jews from slavery in Egypt, the angel of death came and took the first-born of every family. But he passed over the homes of the Jews, who had marked their houses with the blood of a lamb. Today Passover celebrates Jewish freedom with unleavened bread (matzos).

*J*F A POLL were to be taken among Jews, Passover would be chosen the most popular festival. For, gladsome as is Purim, radiant as is Chanukah, charming as is Succos, inspiring as are the holy days, none has that combination of ceremonial loveliness, treasured family associations, springtime exuberance, hallowed national memories and hopes which are contained in Passover.

The holiday probably originated in antiquity as a festival of spring. When the winter months are over and passed, spring bursts into bloom in Palestine. There is none of the slow unfolding of Northern climes. Suddenly the hillsides are covered with red anemones. The fruit trees are in blossom. The sweet fragrance of the acacia stirs the blood of the young and the memories of the old. From the hills of Nazareth, the valley of Jezreel looks like a vast oriental rug woven of fields of golden grain, blossoming almonds, figs and olives and flowers bursting with color from the caresses of the hot sun. The moon has a special brilliance and feeling of closeness. One can read by its light on a spring night in Palestine. Understandably the ancient Israelites who loved their earth and sky could cry out, "The Heavens declare the glory of God; the earth showeth forth the work of His hands."

This exultation found expression in a springtime festival. But the moral genius of the Hebrews was not content with a holiday that had no ethical or historical significance. They transformed this nature festival into a memorial of freedom. According to the account in Genesis, Joseph's brothers and father followed him into Egypt. His forgiveness and his bounty provided for their needs in a time of famine. Then Joseph died, and all that generation. In the course of time, a new Pharaoh arose who "knew not Joseph." He enslaved the Israelites and ordered the destruction of their male babies. One child was hidden in the bulrushes, was found there by Pharaoh's daughter, then was raised in her home as a prince. This youth, Moses, could not endure the oppression of his brethren. After some trials and preparation, he came before Pharaoh to demand his people's freedom. In the name of the stern God he had found in the wilderness he cried, "Let My people go that they may serve Me." After ten dreadful plagues, described vividly in the Book of Exodus, Pharaoh relented. The Israelites fled in haste. There was no time for the leavening of their bread; so it was baked unleavened. Jewish tradition selected this incident for special significance. Jews were required to remove all leaven (*chometz*) from their homes for seven days, and to eat matzos, the unleavened bread of affliction. Passover probably derives its name from the Avenging Angel's passing over the houses of the Israelites when the Egyptian first-born were stricken; although it has some connection also with the Paschal lamb.

Through the ages, Passover has meant many things to the Jews. Its most enduring meaning is suggested by the first of the Ten Commandments—"I am the Lord Thy God. . ." Here is the supreme announcement of all history. But what follows? ". . . who created the heaven and the earth"? No. ". . . who brought forth man, and food to sustain him"? No. The great proclamation of God's being is followed by the words, ". . . who brought thee out of the land of Egypt, out of the house of bondage." From the very beginning, the Jew saw God's hand in history. He owed his very existence as a people to Divine intervention. The Passover ritual relates, "Few in numbers with but seventy souls went thy fathers down into Egypt and now thy God has made thee as numerous as the stars . . . not one only sought to destroy us, but men in all generations; and the Holy One, Blessed be He, saves us from their hands." Note the present tense "saves." Jews may continue to be persecuted, but the Guardian of Israel slumbers not. He will not permit His beloved people to be destroyed.

This is the ultimate meaning of the plagues and of the other miracles described in the Book of Exodus.

59

There are naturalistic explanations of the plagues. In the spring, red clay washes into the Nile making its waters seem like blood. This writer once encountered a storm of locusts in Egypt which completely blackened the sky and prevented all normal activity. Perhaps this happened in a similar natural way in the time of Moses. Possibly there is basis for a moralistic explanation. The talmudic rabbis explained this very plague of darkness in terms of ethics. They say there was darkness from above and darkness from below. The upper darkness was the blindness of the rich who saw not the suffering of the poor. Whereas ignorance and superstition blinded the lower classes, so that "no man saw his brother." This, say the rabbis, was the real plague of darkness, the true tragedy of Egypt. Without minimizing the truth and usefulness of these explanations, the simple fact, according to the Jews, is that God saved them. With an outstretched arm, He carried them safely across the Red Sea while their enemies floundered in its waters. On their behalf He performed miracles; that is the accepted version. This statement must be qualified. The possibility of miracles is accepted by Jewish tradition. However, the belief in miracles is not necessary to validate Jewish doctrines. This may be contrasted with orthodox Christianity which admits that its doctrines stand or fall with the belief in the central miracle of the Christian faith. Jews may or may not believe that God wrought miracles in Egypt. It is immaterial. In either case, the central truths of Judaism are not affected.

When the Jews were exiled from Palestine, when their holy Temple was destroyed, they adapted their institutions to new conditions. This adaptability made survival possible. The agricultural aspects of Passover were de-emphasized; the Temple observances were transferred symbolically to the home. Thus the Seder came into being. The word "seder" literally means order. Actually it means the arrangement of ceremonies on Passover eve. This is a home observance as so many Jewish holidays are, principally. In this way Jewish home life was beautified; family ties were strengthened. Thus divorce, desertion, drunkenness, crimes of violence were little known among the Jews. The sweetness of devoted family life compensated for the world's mistreatment.

Because of its association with the home, the Passover Seder exercised a very strong appeal among the Jews. For this observance the families gather from near and far. Even the prodigal, the cynic, the skeptic returns. The atmosphere is festive; the service includes ancient gay songs and games for the children. The symbols of the first Passover are displayed—the lamb's shankbone, recalling the marks on the Israelites' houses which the Angel of Death passed over; the bitter herbs, a reminder of the bitter hardships of Egyptian bondage; the unleavened bread as a remembrance of the hasty flight to freedom. At a dramatic moment of the service, the door of the house is thrown open for the return of Elijah, the prophet, to bring word of the coming of the Messiah. It is not without significance that the last supper of Jesus was the Seder. In the colorful calendar of the Jew nothing is more quaint, touching or beautiful than the eve of Passover. In his poem "Seder Night," Israel Zangwill suggests the contrast between the external world in which the Jew lived his physical existence and his serene inner life:

> Prosaic miles of streets stretch all around
> Astir with restless, hurried life, and spanned
> By arches that with thunderous trains resound,
> And throbbing wires that galvanize the land;
> Gin-palaces in tawdry splendor stand;
> The newsboys shriek of mangled bodies found;
> The last burlesque is playing in the Strand—
> In modern prose all poetry seems drowned.
> Yet in ten thousand homes this April night,
> An ancient People celebrates its birth
> To Freedom, with a reverential mirth,
> With customs quaint, and many a hoary rite,
> Waiting until, its tarnished glories bright,
> Its God shall be the God of all the earth.

Historically the profoundest meaning of Passover is something which sets Judaism apart from other religions. It marks the birth of a nation. Out of a mass of slaves, Moses fashioned a nation and gave them a faith. From that day to this, Jews have never ceased to be a people. They have not been a sect, a denomination, as are the Christian groups. Common memories, problems, hopes, common attachment to the land of Israel and to the Hebrew language conjoined to common faith have made and kept them a people. Through the centuries this has been taken for granted. In recent years, however, some Reform Jews have questioned it, but events have returned most of them to the historic tradition.

Nationhood was the natural state of the ancient Hebrews in their own land. But what held them together as a people in the Diaspora? Certainly their faith was the principal binding force. By the time of the dispersion their faith was surrounded by a whole rubric of laws and customs which set them apart. Also they had a common experience of persecution which strengthened their sense of group solidarity. They loved Palestine and prayed each day, "Next year in Jerusalem." The Hebrew language was sacred to them; it expressed and sustained their deepest feelings. Beyond these factors was the sense of mission. Jews believed they were the chosen people.

This doctrine has lent itself to much misunderstanding. It has been compared with the German Nazi or the Russian Communist sense of mission. But it has nothing to do with conquest, power, glory. Its classic definition was that of the prophet, a "suffering servant." When the Jews were chosen, they received not a crown but a yoke. "You alone have I known; therefore will I punish you for your iniquities." Theirs was the acceptance of heavier burdens and more exacting duties. The goal was the realization of God's kingdom of justice and truth first in their own nation and then in the life of all humanity. This task required the existence, the continuance, of a living people. The ancient Greeks could produce their sculpture and their literature, and then disappear. Their gifts became and remained the heritage of mankind. But a people that is chosen (or, as some Jewish modernists believe, chose) to be witnesses of the living God, must continue to live. They resist disappearance. They discourage intermarriage. By distinctive beliefs and customs, they remain a distinctive group. This exacts a price, often a terrible price. Most men are not so constituted as to accept differences tolerantly and to use them constructively. What they do not understand, they fear, and what they fear, they hate. And out of fear and hate come persecution and pogroms. Thus, through the centuries the Jews have become what the exilic Isaiah, the molder of the mission idea, prophesied, "the suffering servant."

It might be well at this point to note the difference between the Jewish and the Christian concepts of the suffering servant. According to the Jews, and also to recent Christian historical scholarship, the prophet was depicting the twofold role of the Jewish people, testimony and martyrdom. According to the Christian tradition, the prophet was announcing the coming of Christ. Jews see no reason for crediting the prophet with the anticipation of an event which in their opinion did not occur, namely, the messiahship of Jesus.

Why did the Jews reject Jesus? The answer is that the Jews have never rejected Jesus. We do not know from any contemporary Jewish sources what the Jews thought about the young carpenter from Galilee who died on a hill overlooking Jerusalem. According to modern historical scholarship, the Gospels were written from a generation to a century after his death. These documents were composed by men who could not be regarded as Jews. They were Christian sectarians who despaired of converting the Jews. It was to the Romans that they now turned for converts. This dissatisfaction with the Jews and this desire to win the Romans found expression in the Gospels. Similarly the reference to Christ in the Antiquities of Josephus was written at least half a century after the death of Jesus. Further, most authorities on Josephus regard this as a later interpolation by a zealous Christian editor. It is inconsistent with the other writings of Josephus.

In any event, it can be correctly stated that there is not a single reference to Jesus in any existing Jewish document of his time. Was this a conspiracy of silence? Possibly, but probably not. Those were very turbulent times. The Jews, under the heel of Rome, were seething with discontent and rebelliousness. Zealots rose all over the land. Some believed the world was coming to an end. Others wanted the people to turn their backs on the world. Then there were the fanatical patriots who sought to throw off the foreign yoke. Facing these conditions, Emperor Tiberius sent his most ruthless procurator, Pontius Pilate, to enforce order and obedience on the Jews. The records show that he put thousands of Jews to death for actual or potential rebellion. The names of most of them are unknown. It is quite likely that the crucifixion (which was the common Roman practice) of a young zealot from Galilee was lost in the whole troubled sea of unrecorded suffering.

Only later when Paul fashioned a new religion around Jesus, the Christ, did Jews take cognizance of him. Then they rejected not Jesus, the Jewish teacher, but Christ the Messiah. There were definite criteria for the advent of the Messiah. He was to usher in the messianic kingdom of justice, truth and peace. Not Jesus alone but many other Jews who through the centuries claimed to be the Messiah were judged and found wanting. Wars, oppression, corruption, continued as before. The real Messiah, they believed, was yet to come. As to Jesus in particular, the Jews were especially repelled by the claim that he had fulfilled the law which thenceforth could be disregarded. Paul found this anti-nomism necessary in order to make the new and still Jewish religion palatable to the Romans. How could they be expected to undertake the onerous burden of Jewish laws, 613 of them in the Torah alone? It was announced then that the advent of Christ had cancelled the law. This made the acceptance of the new faith utterly impossible for the Jews to whom the Torah was the foundation of all faith.

Finally, Jews have rejected Christianity because of

the concepts with which the Church fathers buttressed and embellished the new faith in order to make it acceptable to the pagan Roman world. Completely alien to Jewish thought were such ideas as Immaculate Conception, virgin birth, trinitarianism, Holy Ghost, vicarious atonement, the assumption of Jesus (and later of Mary), and the "fall." The religion *of* Jesus was understandable to them; it was Jewish. The religion *about* Jesus was beyond their recognition. They doubted even that Jesus would recognize it.

As the centuries passed, the Jewish attitude toward Jesus was conditioned by another factor, Christian persecution. There was something about the stubborn, unregenerate Jews in their midst which irritated the Christians. So long as Jews proved they could live good, God-fearing lives without Christ, the whole foundation of Christian life was challenged. Only so recently as in March, 1950, the announcement was made of the formation of a new group, The American Committee on the Christian Approach to the Jews. The Home Missions Council, The Foreign Missions Conference and the Federal Council of Churches of Christ in America are represented on the Committee. Its announced twofold program is to combat anti-Semitism and to convert the Jews. The stated reason for the second objective is relevant to our discussion. It rejected the view that Jews should be omitted from missionary efforts on the ground that they worship the same God as the Christians. That view, the statement added, "is to maintain that Judaism, which is without Christ, and in fact rejects and denies Jesus Christ, is adequate for the Jew. This means that the Jew does not need Christ. To admit this would end all motivations for evangelism or Christian missionary effort at home and abroad."

Jews will reject such Christian evangelism as they have in the past. They may also question the morality of this approach—good will at the price of conversion. However, our concern here is with the fact that the persistent loyalty of the Jews to their own faith brought down upon them the irritation, the frustration and finally the persecution of Christendom. It was a Christian pope who first confined the Jews to ghettos and excluded them from normal relations with Christians. It was a Christian church which hounded them with the Inquisition. Down through the centuries innumerable Jews have been vilified, beaten, put to death by Christians acting in the name of Christ. Is it any wonder then that Jews have been unable to regard Jesus with affection, even with objectivity?

In the past generation, however, there has been a wholesale change in attitude. The religious factors in anti-Semitism have become less prominent. Common foes have brought the religions closer together. Jewish emancipation from ghetto-thinking has been advanced. Jews have begun to study the life and teachings of Jesus with greater sympathy. He is included in the curriculum of many progressive religious schools. High-school departments have courses in comparative religion which inform young Jews about the religion of their neighbors. Christian and Jewish clergymen exchange pulpits; Sunday school classes visit each other's houses of worship. Books on Jesus by Jewish authors are appearing with greater frequency; most noteworthy are the popular works of Sholem Asch.

Although no official action has been taken or will be, the net result seems to be the re-inclusion of Jesus in the mainstream of Jewish history. A Jewish basis has been found for most of his teachings. His stature is that of the Hebrew prophet, fearless fighter for righteousness. Like all religious geniuses, he was unique. As with Isaiah and Amos before him, he did not merely echo his people's convictions. Passing through the alchemy of his sensitive soul, the ancient beliefs found a new emphasis; they received the immortal impress of his luminous, loving personality.

However, this should not lead to any mistaken notion about the readiness of Jews to accept Jesus as Christ. Of this there is no indication or any likelihood. How then do Jews feel today about the messianic idea? Here one must distinguish between traditional and modernist Jews. The Orthodox still believe in the coming of a personal Messiah, and pray each day for his advent. A large segment of the liberal Jewish community has discarded the notion of a single messianic personality who is to save mankind. They believe this reflects an earlier stage in the development of religion. In its place they affirm their faith in a messianic era which is to be achieved by the co-operative efforts of good men of all nations, races and religions.

However, whether modernist or traditionalist, two basic elements remain in the messianic outlook of Jews. They received classic expression in the prophet's charge:

> Is it too light a thing that thou shouldest be my servant
> To raise up the tribes of Jacob,
> And to restore the offspring of Israel;
> I will also give thee for a light of the nations,
> That my salvation may be unto the ends of the earth.

With few exceptions, religious Jews today believe as did the prophet twenty-five hundred years ago, in the restoration of Israel and the ultimate redemption of mankind. Further, as Chief Rabbi Hertz wrote, "The restoration of Israel was a necessary prelude to the establishment of God's kingship on earth." The return to Zion is essentially religious in its motivation. It has also proved to be practical humanitarianism. This writer as Adviser on Jewish Affairs to the United States Military Commanders in Europe in 1946 and 1947 did everything in his power to effect the resettlement of the 250,000 Jewish displaced persons in the camps. They were the pathetic survivors of the Nazi extermination program. The combined efforts of the United States State Department, the United Nations, UNRRA, I.R.O., the Jewish and non-sectarian humanitarian agencies could not open doors anywhere, not even in the United States to any substantial numbers. Only when Israel became a sovereign state and took immigration into its own hands, was the problem solved. Hundreds of thousands of Jews swiftly came to its hospitable shores. There was one month alone in which more Jews entered Israel than all the other countries of the world had admitted in a period of years. The quick liquidation of the Jewish D.P. problem, among others, is concrete evidence of the practical statesmanship of the return to Zion.

Basically, however, Zionism is not a program for the solution of refugee problems. It is a religiously motivated undertaking for the restoration of the remnant of Israel to its ancestral homeland. The Preamble to the Draft Constitution of the new state proclaims:

WE, THE PEOPLE OF ISRAEL,
HUMBLY giving thanks to Almighty God for having delivered us from the burden of exile and brought us back to our ancient land;
RECALLING the tenacious endurance of the generations of the Exile and their heroic sacrifices for the survival of our people and the preservation of its spiritual heritage;
RESOLVED to rebuild our Commonwealth in accordance with the ideals of peace and righteousness of the Prophets of Israel, to welcome home every Jew who seeks entry, and to promote the security and well-being of all who dwell within our gates,
HAVE ADOPTED THE FOLLOWING CONSTITUTION:

71

There are various political parties, philosophies and trends in Israel. But the backbone of the country are the Chalutzim, the pioneers returning to build and to defend. A. D. Gordon, the spokesman of these pioneers who sought not only the return to Zion but also a return to the soil, said, "We were the first to proclaim that man was made in the image of God. Now we must say, 'The nation must be created in the image of God.'" Mr. David Ben Gurion, labor leader and prime minister of the nation which Gordon envisioned, stated before the Israeli Bar Association on June 6, 1949, that the laws of Israel will be based on the dual principles of the "gathering of the exiles" and "love thy neighbor as thyself." The first, he said, was dictated by need. The second was "inherent in Israel's universal mission." There is a profound mystic conviction that through the return to Zion, Jews will again make a contribution to mankind. Nearly four thousand years ago a tribe emerged from the desert and attached itself to the soil of Palestine. This union of land and people received a divine blessing. From it came Moses and Jesus, Judaism and Christianity, the Ten Commandments and the Sermon on the Mount. Is it too much to hope that the return of this persistent people to that sacred soil may again yield new insights, healing, hope to the troubled children of men? Is it beyond the range of possibility that Israel may even be a bridge between East and West?

Perhaps this very hope is an indication of the second

enduring trend in the Jewish messianic outlook. The Jews are, in the prophet's arresting phrase, "Prisoners of Hope." The Jewish outlook is by its very nature optimistic, progressive, forward-looking. Occasionally one encounters an almost completely de-Judaized Jew who poses Hamlet's question. But the typical Jew, steeped in the traditions of his people, does not question the future; he takes it for granted. Even in the D.P. camps of Germany, where Jews had every right to doubt the wisdom of bringing more Jewish children into the world, the birth rate was the highest to be found among Jews anywhere.

This hopefulness is a product of the long view of history. A people that has endured so much knows that it can survive more. It flows from the faith in a good God whose ways may sometimes be obscure but whose justice is ultimately triumphant. It prods Jews constantly to strive for a better world, to be in the thick and at the front of movements for social reform. Even the very Jewish radical who may ignore his Jewishness is the product of its messianic fervor. Whether they could articulate this belief or not, most Jews in their hearts would say "Amen" to the ringing conclusion of the prize-winning address on "The Mission of the Jew" which was delivered in an Indiana oratorical contest in 1918. The speaker was a De Pauw University student named David E. Lilienthal who was destined to become head of the Tennessee Valley Authority and the Atomic Energy Commission. Young Lilienthal concluded, "And so shall be accomplished my people's uplifting task, by the spirit of the Lord, who keeps aflame in this Messiah nation the passion for their mission, the Unity of God, the unity of man."

In a very real sense this messianic idealism derives from Passover. The holiday is even known as Zeman Cherusenu—the season of our freedom. The very use of the form "our" shows the intent which was to make every Jew in all ages feel as if he personally had been liberated. The corollary, to free mankind, was also stated in the Torah and was subsequently elaborated and concretized by the prophets.

This first great mass emancipation of recorded history has taken hold not only of the memories of Jews but of the imagination of mankind. It played a role in the American Revolution. On the very day when independence was declared, a seal was selected for the new nation by a committee consisting of Franklin, Adams and Jefferson. The design represented the Egyptians drowning in the Red Sea, as Moses was leading the Israelites to freedom. The inscription read, "Rebellion against tyrants is obedience to God."

On the American Liberty Bell is an utterance not of Washington but of Moses. "Proclaim liberty throughout the land to all the inhabitants thereof." It may be safely said that after this first liberation men were never content again to be in chains.

74

Shavuos

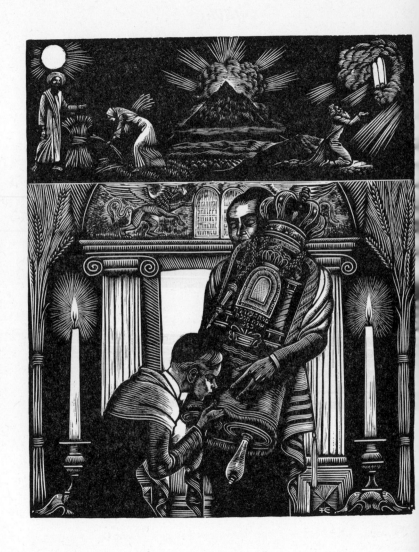

Shavuos

This holy day originally marked the end of the Palestinian grain harvest (top left of woodcut); later God's giving of the Torah to Moses (top right). Today most Reform congregations and many Conservative synagogues conduct Confirmation exercises on Shavuos. This ceremony, for both boys and girls, is a development from the traditional Bar Mitzvah, when boys on reaching the age of thirteen are considered sufficiently adult to fulfill the laws of the Torah.

THERE is a seeming paradox in the principal scripture readings prescribed for the festival of Shavuos. The central theme of the holiday is enunciated in the twentieth chapter of the Book of Exodus. Here is described the giving of the Ten Commandments through Moses to the Hebrew people. Henceforth this is their law, their mission, their destiny. This is their constitution as a separate people. "The Law which Moses commanded us is the heritage of the congregation of Jacob."

But the same holiday also requires the reading of the Book of Ruth. And the central figure of this idyllic story is a gentile. How do we reconcile this broad tolerance with the apparent particularism of the Torah?

Ruth is a Moabite woman who has married the son of Naomi. The Hebrew mother decides to return to Canaan after the death of both her sons. She bids farewell to her widowed daughters-in-law. Orpah goes her way, but Ruth refuses to forsake the older woman. "Entreat me not to leave thee, or to return from following after thee; for whither thou goest, I will go; and where thou lodgest, I will lodge; thy people shall be my people, and thy God my God: where thou diest, will I die, and there will I be buried."

Ruth accompanies Naomi, later marries Boaz, and becomes the progenitor of King David from whose royal line it is believed the Messiah must come. Thus it is a non-Jew, a proselyte, who plays such a crucial role in Jewish history and Jewish hopes.

What then is the attitude of Jews toward conversion? If Jews believe their religion is the truth or even that it possesses necessary insights for mankind, why do they not seek to win others to it? The answer is that Jews have always accepted converts, but have never especially sought them. Ruth was only one of the innumerable men and women who have come into the Jewish fold. Even the wife of Moses was the daughter of a Midianite priest. The Book of Esther relates, "Many of the people of the Persian empire were converted to Judaism." The classical writers report that a number of high-born Romans adopted the Jewish faith. Matthew writes of the Jews, "Ye compass land and sea to make one proselyte." An entire Yemenite host was converted to Judaism in the sixth century. In the year 750, the Kuzari tribesmen and their King Bulan became Jews. The Falashas of Abyssinia are the products of mixed marriages between Jews and Negroes who accepted Judaism. Most American rabbis can testify to the number of conversions that they are requested to perform, usually in relation to intermarriages.

The classic statement on proselytes appears in the Talmud:

"Our Rabbis taught: If at the present time a man desires to become a proselyte, he is to be addressed as follows: What reason have you for desiring to become a proselyte; do you not know that the people of Israel are persecuted and oppressed, harassed and overcome with afflictions? If he replies, I know and yet I desire to be a Jew, he is accepted forthwith and is given instruction in some of the minor and some of the major commandments. He is not to be persuaded or dissuaded too much. If he accepts he is regarded as a full member of the house of Israel in all respects."

The doors have always been open. Why have the Jews not sought to bring crowds of converts through them into the house of living Judaism? The basic reason is to be found in the attitude of the Jews toward religion. It was suggested by a German writer who said, *"Wir Juden haben keine religion, wir haben das Judentum."* Judaism is the sum total of the spiritual creativity of the Jewish people. It is not a scheme of salvation. If by accepting certain doctrines men can be delivered from sin, and saved for eternal bliss in the world to come, it is the obvious duty of those who already hold these beliefs to try to save them. But Judaism is a life-long process of education and self-discipline. One cannot be suddenly converted to such a process. He accepts it as a long continuing responsibility with no sure rewards other than in the process itself. "The reward of the good life is the good life."

Furthermore, as the title of a popular Jewish comedy admits, "It is hard to be a Jew." Why should one urge non-Jews to accept the burdens of anti-Semitism, except perhaps for the reason given by the rabbis—"It is better to be among the persecuted than among the persecutors." But this argument is more appealing in literature than in life. The sensible Jewish mind saw no purpose in persuading gentiles to endure discrimination, persecution, genocide, when, without embracing Judaism, they could achieve their rightful place in God's kingdom. By living up to the seven basic laws of ethics and religion as commanded to all men by Adam and Noah, any human being is deemed righteous in the sight of God.

Beyond these logical reasons there is a profounder cause which transcends logic. The Jews possess a deep, instinctual drive for self-preservation as a people. Whenever their group survival is threatened, a powerful resistance is set up. Intuitively, then, they do not encourage an undertaking which might bring many believers to Judaism but overwhelm the Jewish people. Professor Klausner of Jerusalem's great Hebrew University in his penetrating volume on Jesus suggests this

80

as one reason for the Jewish rejection of early Christianity; by denying the on-going validity of the Torah as the constitution of the Jewish nation it would have brought about the dissolution and disappearance of the Jews as a distinctive group. Always this has been resisted.

On the other hand the desire to win the world to Jewish religious and ethical ideals has been a cardinal element in Judaism. Almost every major test of the patriarchs, the founders of the Jewish people, is followed by the command, "Be thou a blessing." Whether it be Abraham's readiness to offer his son, Isaac, or Jacob's struggle with the angel, the triumphant demonstration of faith leads immediately to the obligation to serve. In some strange way which Jews regard as Divine selection, this desert tribe was given new insight into the meaning of the universe; they broke through the barriers of the finite and caught a vision of God. It did not let them rest. They felt that they had to bring this light to the nations. "And it shall come to pass" is one of the most frequent and significant phrases in the Bible. It is the confident expression that in God's own time the revelation received by the Jews would find realization in the good life for all mankind, God's kingdom. For this objective the acceptance of Jewish ideas was desired, not necessarily induction into the Jewish religion. Jews seek to win mankind to the ideas of one God, one humanity, the Golden Rule, justice for the oppressed, compassion for the unfortunate, but make

81

no special efforts to convert non-Jews to the specific rubric of Judaism.

This concept of the Jewish mission is magnificently expressed in the Olenu prayer which is recited in Jewish services:

May the time not be distant, O God, when Thy name shall be worshipped in all the earth, when unbelief shall disappear and error be no more. Fervently we pray that the day may come when all men shall invoke Thy name, when corruption and evil shall give way to purity and goodness, when superstition shall no longer enslave the mind, nor idolatry blind the eye, when all who dwell on earth shall know that to Thee alone every knee must bend and every tongue give homage. O may all, created in Thine image, recognize that they are brethren, so that, one in spirit and one in fellowship, they may be forever united before Thee. Then shall Thy kingdom be established on earth and the word of Thine ancient seer be fulfilled: The Lord shall reign forever and ever.

We return now to the principal event commemorated by Shavuos. The day is known as Yom Mattan Torah, the day of the giving of the Torah on Mount Sinai. There are differences of opinion about the origins and development of the law. But there is no difference about the centrality of Torah in Jewish history; nor should there be any doubt that at some moment of history these revolutionary insights, which may be called the will of God, were revealed to this remarkable people.

Jewish tradition records that they were given to Moses
on Sinai.

This epochal event evoked from the Jews their exultation and poetic imagination. The rigors of the law
were tempered by fanciful legends with moral meanings. Sometimes we learn more from them about the
soul of the Jew than from systematic statements of fact.
For example, the Midrash relates that when the first
words of the First Commandment were uttered, "I am
the Lord," the whole earth stood still. Not a bird sang,
not a leaf stirred. This was the rabbis' way of saying that
an event had occurred which would change the world.

They say too that the words were issued simultaneously in seventy languages. Thus they stressed the
universal binding character of the ten commandments.
They were not meant for Israel alone but for all mankind.

According to rabbinic lore, the angels protested.
"Man is impure, unreliable; he will not fulfill the Commandments. But we are holy and ever-faithful. Pray,
give us the Torah; we will always obey it." "For that
reason," replied the Almighty, "I will not give it to you.
You do not need my law. But man cannot live without
it." Not perfection, said the rabbis, but the right way;
not sure knowledge of the final rewards, but enough
light to see God's way is what man needs. It is sufficient
to know what God requires of us, that we do justly, love
mercy and walk humbly with Him. The final decisions,
the latter days, are in His hands. To stumbling mankind,

dim in sight, weak-willed, lacking in wisdom, the Torah is a staff of life; it is a fount of living waters; its ways are ways of pleasantness; all its paths lead to peace.

This reverence for the Torah was natural when the Jews lived in their own land, for the law provided necessary regulations in civil as well as religious matters. The Torah was indispensable also when, for many centuries, Jews lived as a segregated community in strange lands. Excluded from normal relations with non-Jews, they established their own life based on Jewish law. The emancipation of the Jews created new problems. "Liberty, Equality, Fraternity" was the slogan of the French Revolution. Jews rushed out of the ghettos pathetically eager for the new life. Looking back from the middle of the twentieth century with memories of Nazi gas chambers still fresh, some writers regard this emancipation as a sham. It offered the Jews, they claim, a spurious equality for the surrender of their heritage. Napoleon set the pattern when he summoned a Sanhedrin to instruct Jews to give up their laws in return for free and equal French citizenship. But how free or equal was a citizenship which denied a minority the right to follow its own religious laws? Emancipation, however, was not to be denied. In Western Europe and in America, Jews soon found themselves in the general community. They shared its life and were influenced by its thought. They desired its advantages for themselves and for their children.

This raised very troublesome questions for a people

84

to whom the Torah had been the basis of all of life. What should they do about the Sabbath? Sunday was the day of rest among Christians. Now that they shared the general life including its economy, how could they avoid normal activity on Saturday? When all Jews lived in a tight little ghetto, there was no problem of travel on the day of rest. But in Berlin or London, in New York or Cincinnati, this problem was much more complicated. Further, travel in the modern world did not involve the actual labor which was required when men used camels or horses. And was turning on a gas jet or flicking an electric switch really the kind of fire-lighting the Torah intended to forbid? Then there was the problem of food. How could Jews associate normally with Christians if they could not break bread together? Observant Jews could not eat in Christian homes or public restaurants for the food was not prepared according to ritual law.

Many other regulations made Jews uncomfortable in the modern world. Did the men have to continue to wear beards? Must women really be separated from men; be placed in synagogue balconies behind screens in religious services?

These problems evoked a variety of answers. One group of Jews simply discarded the Torah and went their merry way. They ceased to be religious Jews in any sense. They solved the problem by denying its existence.

Another element deliberately re-created a ghetto.

They turned their backs upon emancipation. They repudiated the non-Jewish world. They associated exclusively with Jews. They lived in completely Jewish neighborhoods near synagogues, Jewish parochial schools, Kosher butchers; for all practical purposes they reestablished the conditions which Jews had been given the opportunity to escape.

Another segment of Jewry reached the conclusion that an authentic Jewish life was impossible in a free, non-Jewish society. The only place where Jews could live a life that was both completely Jewish and completely free was Palestine. These Jews forsook the Western world and settled in the land of their fathers. This idea received fresh impetus from the establishment of the Jewish state. It placed the destiny of the Jews in their own hands. No longer was migration to Zion a remote dream. Those who meant business could quickly arrange it. Actually, they could fly from New York to Jerusalem in twenty-four hours. This led one provocative writer, Arthur Koestler, to advise American Jews either to settle in Israel if they wanted to live Jewish lives or to give up their Jewishness. Why maintain a purposeless separatism, he asks. Return to Zion or disappear, is his advice.

However, most Western Jews, and this primarily means American Jews, for the United States contains the one really large Jewish community in the Western world, accept none of the above patterns. They turn their backs upon neither the modern world nor their

86

own inheritance. They feel genuinely rooted in American life and they also desire to perpetuate the Jewish heritage, adapted to the modern world. How do they meet the problem of adjusting an old faith to a new life?

The answers fall into three basic patterns, Orthodox, Reform and Conservative. The Orthodox Jew uncompromisingly insists on the authority of revealed law. The Torah is as binding to him as it was to the Israelites at Sinai. And not only the Torah but the fence that was built around the Torah. He submits also to the codes which subsequently adapted Mosaic law to changing conditions. Always the law is central and supreme. Any deviation from it, he believes, would undermine the foundations of Judaism. Through obedience to the law, the Orthodox Jew achieves and maintains personal piety, Jewish identification, clear direction in his religious life and the fulfillment of his sense of duty.

However, Orthodoxy faces the same problems in the modern world as do the other branches of Judaism. It seeks to meet them through a series of practical measures which involve no sacrifice of principle. First, it is producing a new generation of modern, American-trained rabbis. In fact, the Orthodox seminaries are together graduating more rabbis each year than are the institutions training leaders for the Conservative or the Reform rabbinate. These men compare well in general education, culture and ability with their non-Orthodox colleagues. Many of those who served in the chaplaincy in World War II made excellent records. They displayed both adaptability and courageous conviction. As these rabbis penetrate into the communities of America, they make their presence felt.

The Orthodox worship has been modernized without basic compromises of law. Synagogues have been made physically attractive. Decorum has replaced the homey informality which once prevailed. The rabbis preach in English so that young people will understand them. Most modern Orthodox synagogues now conduct late Friday evening services at an hour convenient for all. Increasingly their schools have attractive classrooms and capable teachers.

Nevertheless, the Orthodox Jew in America still finds himself in a Procrustean bed, and he is uncomfortable. How can he adjust his life in the new world to fixed regulations which developed in the old world? One interesting answer emerges from the new State of Israel. Rabbi Judah Maimon, Israel's Minister of Religions, has proposed the convoking of a Sanhedrin. In the days of the Second Temple, a supreme court was set up consisting of seventy-one priests and scholars who adjudicated cases on the basis of the Torah. This court was empowered to adapt the law to changing conditions. When Napoleon sought to emancipate Jews from their ancient laws, he ordered the convening of a Sanhedrin. This body failed because it could not act freely but was compelled to obey the will of the emperor. But Napoleon, some believed, was on the right track. Only a Sanhedrin would have the authority to unfreeze Jewish law.

Rabbi Maimon's first attempts seemed premature but they may bear fruit. A new generation both in Israel and the United States may make some such historic step necessary. In any event, the authority of revealed law will remain the foundation of Judaism for the Orthodox Jews.

The Reform Jew approached his problem differently. His thinking was influenced originally by German Protestantism and German rationalism. These encouraged him to question and revaluate his tradition. If Luther could reject the absolute authority of the Vatican, why must progressive German Jews accept the entire structure of Jewish law as eternally binding? Why should they also not return to the Bible and seek out their own truths? Authority then passed from an established institution to the individual conscience.

Reform Judaism came to America in the middle years of the nineteenth century. Under the leadership of Isaac M. Wise, it achieved in this country its greatest strength. Here the pioneering spirit encouraged Reform Jews to depart from the old ways and blaze their own trails. They found America friendly and free. Why should they perpetuate unnecessary differences? The rabbis began to pray in English. The men uncovered their heads in worship. The dietary laws were ignored. Sunday services were introduced. America became their new Jerusalem. Why continue to pray for the restoration of Zion?

This American Judaism had some valuable features. It was in keeping with the times. It retained the loyalty of many young, thoughtful and social-minded Jews who otherwise would have been lost to Judaism entirely. It improved relations with non-Jews, for this kind of religion was understandable to them.

Intrinsically also Reform possessed considerable merit. Its emphasis on prophetic Judaism as contrasted with legal regulations resulted in genuine social zeal among its followers. They were generous in philanthropy and established modern eleemosynary institutions. They participated actively in movements for the common good. Their emphasis on the evolutionary character of Judaism was essentially sound. They enriched the liturgy as it had always been enriched, by prayers growing out of their own experience. They produced a leadership which moved into the forefront of American religious life.

In time, however, they discovered they had made a grave mistake. They had almost thrown out the baby with the bath water. Experience taught them that Judaism was more than rational ideas and ethical principles. They had lost the poetry, the warmth, the disciplines which characterized the religion of their fathers. It was an attenuated Judaism which they were transmitting to their children. The early Reformers, themselves the product of European Jewishness, possessed considerable knowledge and piety; their children had little; their grandchildren less.

Then a new development occurred. A great wave of East European Jews had poured into this country in

90

the last quarter of the nineteenth century. These Jews were Orthodox or Yiddishists or Socialists. But some of their children became Reform Jews. A number of their most gifted sons became Reform rabbis. At a time when Reform was becoming conscious of its weaknesses these Jews poured new life's blood into its veins. Most noteworthy among these re-Judaizers of Reform was Stephen S. Wise, outstanding American rabbi of the first half of the twentieth century. He was the founder of the Free Synagogue of New York, the Jewish Institute of Religion, and the World Jewish Congress. He was both a pioneer and an example of new trends in American Jewish life, moving toward a return to Zionism, identification with world Jewry, and the resurrection of tradition.

In the course of little over a generation, the character of Reform Judaism has changed. At present the larger part of the membership and the rabbinate of Reform temples are descended from East European Jews. Many basic customs have been re-established. All but a handful of congregations now conduct Friday evening services and encourage traditional Sabbath observances in the home. Holiday ceremonials have been re-established and embellished. Most Reform families now conduct Sedorim in their homes. Weekday Hebrew schools are to be found in most temples. Bar Mitzvah is again a common practice. Yizkor memorial prayers are recited for the dead.

The net result has been the revitalization of Reform

Judaism. In the five years ending at the mid-century, over one hundred new congregations were founded, so that a total of five hundred is rapidly being approached. The congregations have experienced a great growth. Some now have a membership of over two thousand families. Reform has become dynamically Jewish, without sacrifice of its inherent liberalism.

But what about Torah? Some Reform laymen and many Reform rabbis have felt the need for a codification of Jewish law. They maintain that the present situation in which every congregation and every rabbi, in fact every man, woman and child, decide what to observe and what not to observe is anarchic. They say that it is impossible now to give clear answers to the most elementary questions about belief and practice. They point to the difficulty of perpetuating a religion that is so amorphous. They demand some minimal code of faith and observance.

However, this group seems to represent a minority view. The majority find in the very flexibility of Reform Judaism its strength. They indicate that a basic pattern of observances has emerged; that the need, the beauty and the usefulness of traditional ceremonies are winning adherents without the use of compulsion. As one prominent spokesman said, "There is no need to codify our contrivances." It appears that Reform Judaism will have a recognizable religious pattern created spontaneously out of necessity and desire, and not through a sense of ritual obligation.

92

Conservative Judaism is a midway house. Late arrival on the American scene gave it certain advantages. It could clearly see the earlier mistakes made by Reform and could try to avoid them. Consisting almost entirely of East European Jews seeking adjustment to American conditions, it started with sources of strength which German rationalism had dissipated. The Conservative movement, aiming for adaptation without unnecessary sacrifice of tradition, grew rapidly. Although never equalling the number of Reform congregations and rabbis, its rate of expansion was at least as great. Lively Conservative congregations, usually with progressive schools, were established in every community with a considerable Jewish population. An important seminary with high standards of scholarship was wisely founded in New York which was becoming the world center of Jewish life. Its graduates coming from backgrounds similar to those of most Reform rabbis soon achieved a similar place in the American community.

Conservatism which has experienced a healthy development is also plagued by the problem of Jewish law. Some of its leaders, the traditionalists, are inflexible in their loyalty to the authority of the Torah, and also to later legal regulations. However, a new generation has arisen which finds much of Jewish law irrelevant to American life. They are worried about the moral effects of the contradictions between expressed beliefs and actual practices. They know, for example, that many of their members ride on the Sabbath, actually ride to the synagogue. Should this dichotomy which easily becomes hypocrisy be permitted to continue or should the entire problem of riding on the Sabbath be resolutely reopened? This is the type of question which is agitating Conservatism without as yet any clear answers for the movement as a whole.

Within the movement, however, a radical wing has developed. The Reconstructionist group is revaluating Jewish law and practice. Some of its leaders maintain that "law no longer belongs in Judaism . . . the regulation of human affairs by judicial processes pertains to the state and not to the synagogue." They do not approve the manipulation of Old World codes to find some justification for New World practices. They desire rather to revitalize the major institutions of Jewish life which gave rise to such practices.

It is hard to find much difference between the approach of this Conservative group and the views of the present majority of tradition-minded Reform rabbis. In fact, proposals have been offered for the merger of Reform and Conservative Judaism. At present these seem premature; too many historic differences still prevail. Another generation, however, is likely to find these divergencies inconsequential. Already there is little observable difference between the actual personal practices of many Reform and Conservative Jews.

Am Yisrael Chai

THIS panorama of the American Jewish scene reveals lights and shadows. Much that made European Judaism so rich and so glorious seems to be gone forever. Jewish life has been immeasurably impoverished. However, a new Judaism is emerging which shows signs of vigorous health. It is indigenous to America and reflects the quality of life here. It demonstrates that American Jews have their roots deeply planted in this country and intend to remain here. Strong sentiment will attach them to Israel. They will give the new state their help and will get much from it in return. But this will be their home, and they will have a thriving Jewish community here. They will be repeating an ancient pattern. In the days of the Second Commonwealth great Jewish communities flourished outside of Palestine as well. Alexandrian Jewry was a notable example. There is good reason now to believe that strong Jewish communities in America and Israel will develop simultaneously and will fructify each other.

"Am Yisrael Chai" is the title of a popular Israeli song. It is also the conclusion of the matter, "The People Israel lives." Despite persecution and decimation, the Jews have survived in the modern world. And despite the blandishments of assimilation and the oppression of dictators, they have emerged with amazing vitality. The new State of Israel is bursting with energy. A healthy self-criticism, bold experimentation and vigorous activity characterize the American Jewish community.

Is there a meaning to this survival? The author gave his answer, and in a sense it is the summation of all he has written in this book, in the charge which he delivered at the Bar Mitzvah of his son, Stephen, amid the ruins of Frankfurt, Germany, on January 25, 1947:

"This is an extraordinary Bar Mitzvah.

"Stephen chose it so. He had been trained for his Confirmation in Rochester during the month of November, but when he learned that my responsibilities would keep me here longer he decided to postpone the event, to learn a new portion and to have the service far from his own friends and our families in the normal, peaceful environment of our community, so as to share it with me and with you. You will forgive me, therefore, a pardonable sense of gratification and pride on this blessed occasion.

"This must be also a very extraordinary and heart-stirring event for many of the Jews who are here this morning. The very fact that no Bar Mitzvah has been held in Frankfurt since 1940, the very fact that since liberation there was not a single Jewish boy in this once great city of Frankfurt who reached the age of thirteen, tells more forcefully than I could dare put into words what happened to the Jewish children. This very building in which we gather was once a Jewish school, alive with the voices and activities of Jewish boys and girls. Stephen, then, becomes the symbol of the childhood that was and is no more.

"This must be a poignant occasion, also, for the surviving members of the Jewish community of Frankfurt. This was one of the great Jewish communities of the world. The Judaism of Frankfurt, which combined the noblest of our tradition with modern enlightenment, was renowned throughout the world. The very fact that we could find no adequate standing synagogue in which to conduct this ceremony reveals the fate of Judaism here. Frankfurt was the home of great Jewish families who combined material success and patriotism with devotion to their faith. Here the Rothschild family flourished. Here the Speyer family made possible the modern University of Frankfurt. From this community came Dr. Paul Ehrlich who helped mankind toward freedom from one of its most devastating scourges.

"It is of special significance that this hall in which we meet was the last institution used by the Jewish community for religious services from 1942 until liberation by the American Army. On November 10, 1938, the synagogues of Frankfurt were desecrated, burned, de-

97

stroyed. The Jewish community then conducted its services in this hall of this school. Here, in these bitter years between 1938 and 1942, with ominous, black clouds gathering overhead and irresistibly pressing down upon them, the remaining members of this community assembled to worship God according to the traditions of their fathers, and to seek strength to withstand their oppressors, and to find solace for their losses.

"But, in the fall of 1942, the end came. Then began the deportations to Litzmannstadt, Lodz, where they were imprisoned in the ghetto and, ultimately, exterminated. At this point, services were discontinued in the Philantropin Building. There was a brief period of a few weeks when they were conducted in a private home. Then the Gestapo ordered them to cease entirely. For three years there were no Jewish religious exercises in Frankfurt, save for the anguished prayers that must have welled up from the hearts of the miserable, terror-stricken people.

"Even the very physical circumstances under which we meet today are extraordinary. This is now a hospital for German war-wounded. Some of the very men who participated in these dreadful things are now round-about. There is a window in which the Magen David, the Star of David, has been defaced by some Nazi hand.

"Yes, we are surrounded by memories today, by tragic memories of a greatness that was and is no more, and of a people who are no longer among the living.

98

"But, that is of the past. The very fact that we are gathered here to worship this morning is a source of hope for the future. On every side you see the wages of the terrible sin which was here committed by the mighty and the wicked. Our eyes confirm the rightness of the prophetic words which Stephen just read to us:

> For the sword hath devoured round about thee.
> Why is the strong one overthrown?
> He stood not because the Lord did thrust him down.

"The oppressor may triumph for a moment. He may enjoy for a short time the rewards of his gangsterism, but his house is built on sand. It cannot stand against the wrath of the Lord. It cannot withstand the irresistible moral laws of history. But Israel survives. This very Bar Mitzvah in these very extraordinary circumstances demonstrates the indestructibility of our people and our faith. 'Am Yisrael Chai.'

"In the prophetic portion that was just read, the Lord says, 'Fear not, for I am with thee.' That is a magnificent promise and an imperishable source of hope. It is also justification for pride. It makes me proud I am a Jew. Despite the misfortunes of my people, I would not exchange that heritage for anything in the world.

"It is this heritage which we formally transmit to you today, Stephen. When I place my hands upon your head in benediction, I will be the humble instrument through which will flow the stream of history and memories of the great and the good in Israel, the ideals and the aspirations of our people, the strength and the lift of our faith. It is something which places upon you a solemn responsibility to be worthy of its precepts, to be loyal to its ideals, and to express them in a life of service.

" 'So be the Lord with you as I will let you go.' "